Love Coloring Book

Positive Quotes and Affirmations

from Popular Love Songs

Love Coloring Book

Positive Quotes and Affirmations from Popular Love Songs

CAMPTYS INSPIRATIONS

© Copyright Camptys Inspirations - All rights reserved.

The content contained in this book may not be reproduced, duplicated or transmitted without direct written permission from the author or publisher.

The inspirational quotes are the intellectual property of Andrea Campbell

ISBN: 978-1-914997-42-6

Pocket Learner Publishing

This coloring book belongs to:

_____

All that you are is all that I'll ever need

—*Ed Sheeran*

And I can't help but stare, 'cause I see truth somewhere in your eyes

—Justin Timberlake

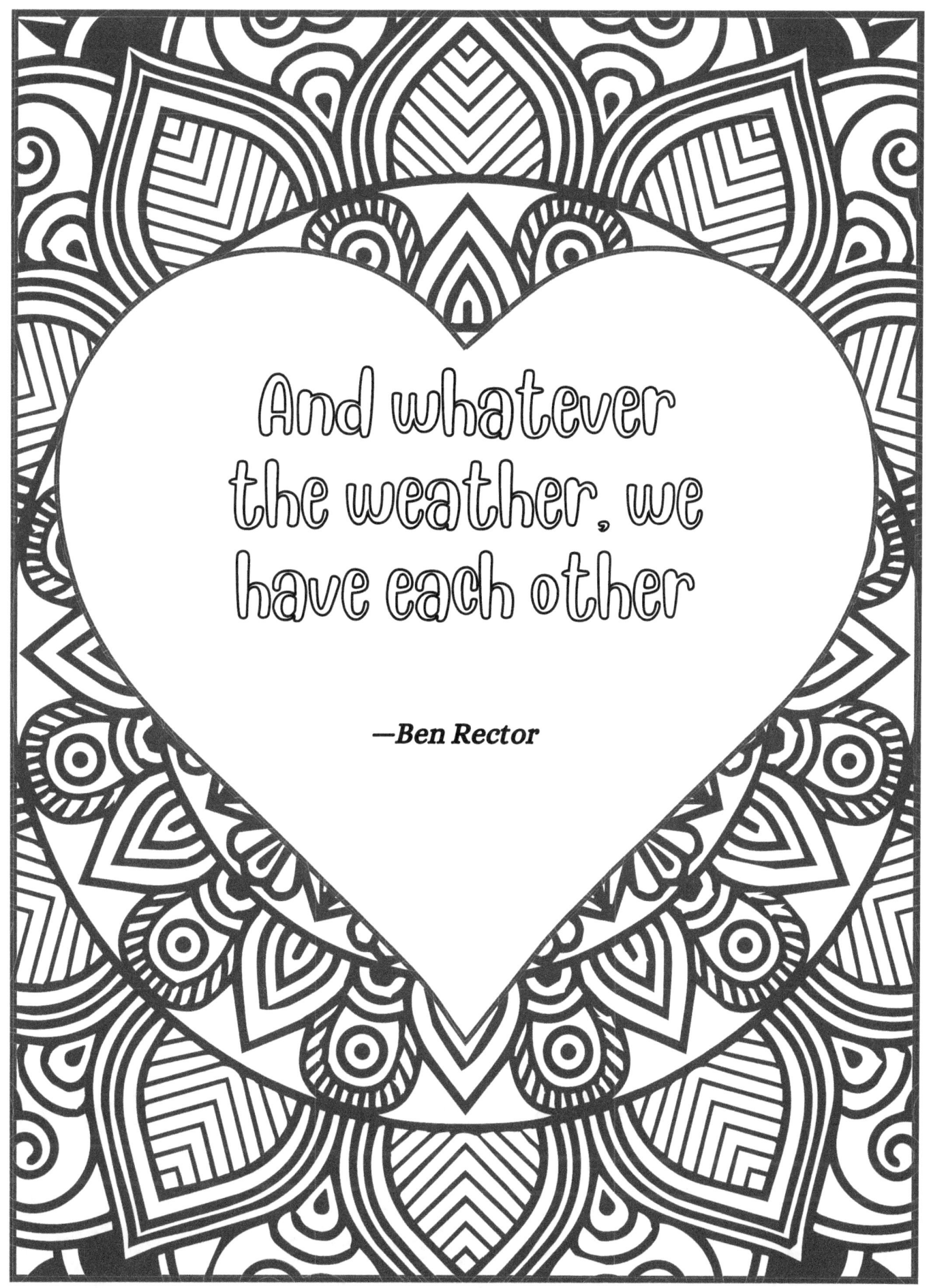

At long last, love has arrived
And I thank God I'm alive

—Frankie Valli

I love you more than I have ever found a way to say to you

—Ben Folds

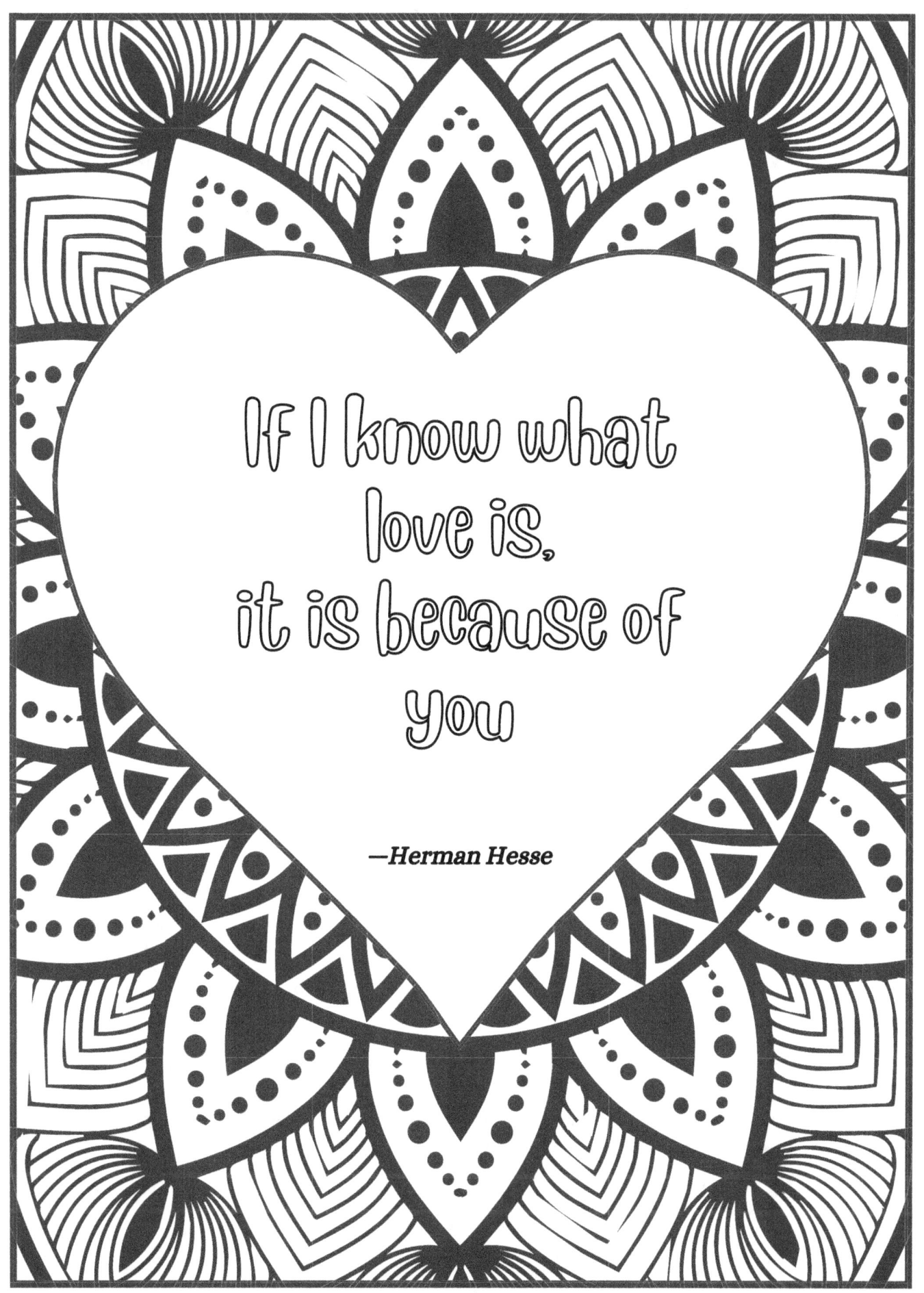

If I know what love is,
it is because of you

—Herman Hesse

In this story I am the Poet. You're the Poetry

—Arzum Unzun

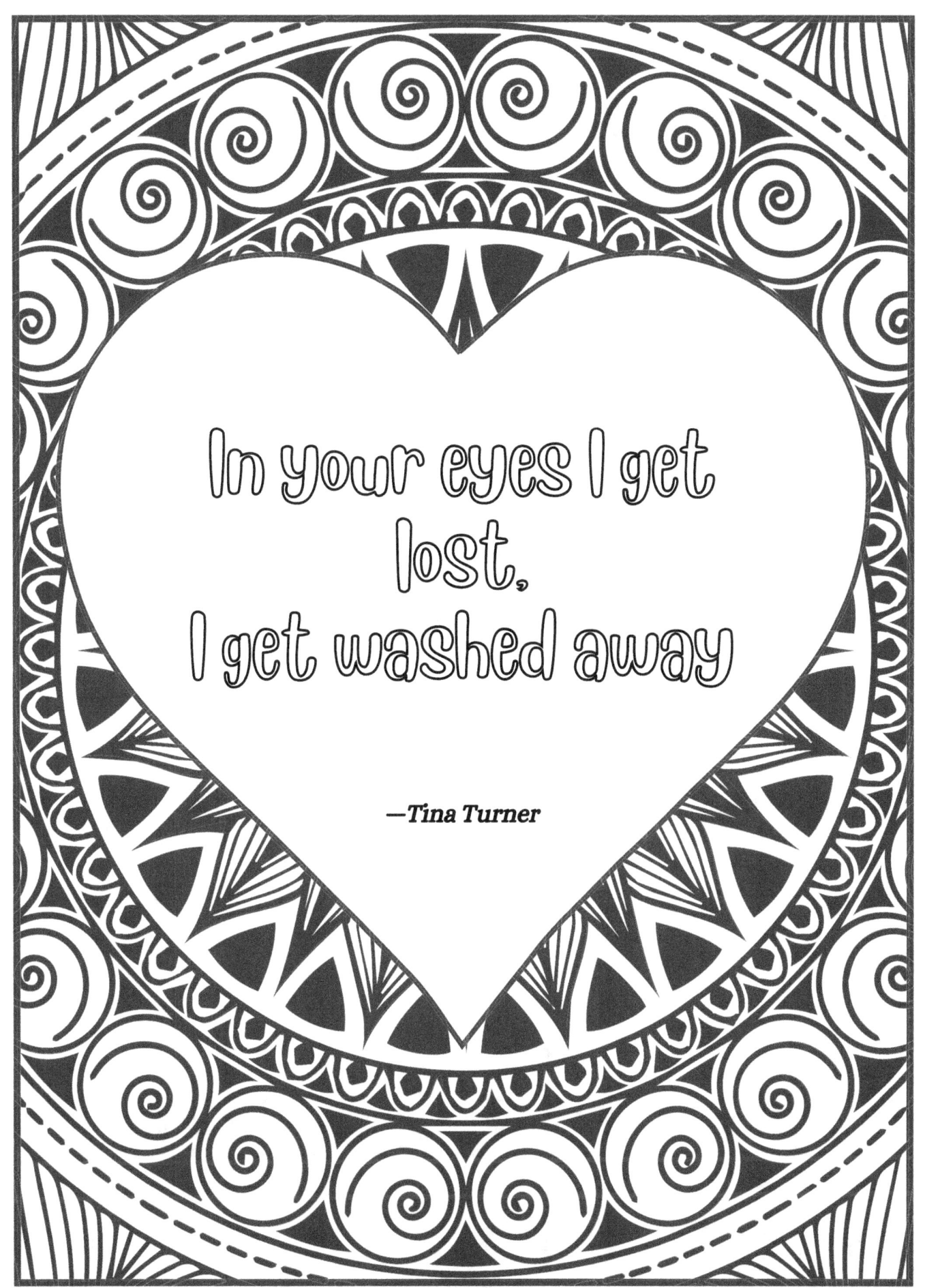

Out of all the people in the world, I just can't believe you're mine

—*Air Supply*

Two hearts that beat as one, Our lives have just begun

—Diana Ross & Lionel Richie

With all my heart, I love you baby

—Anita Baker

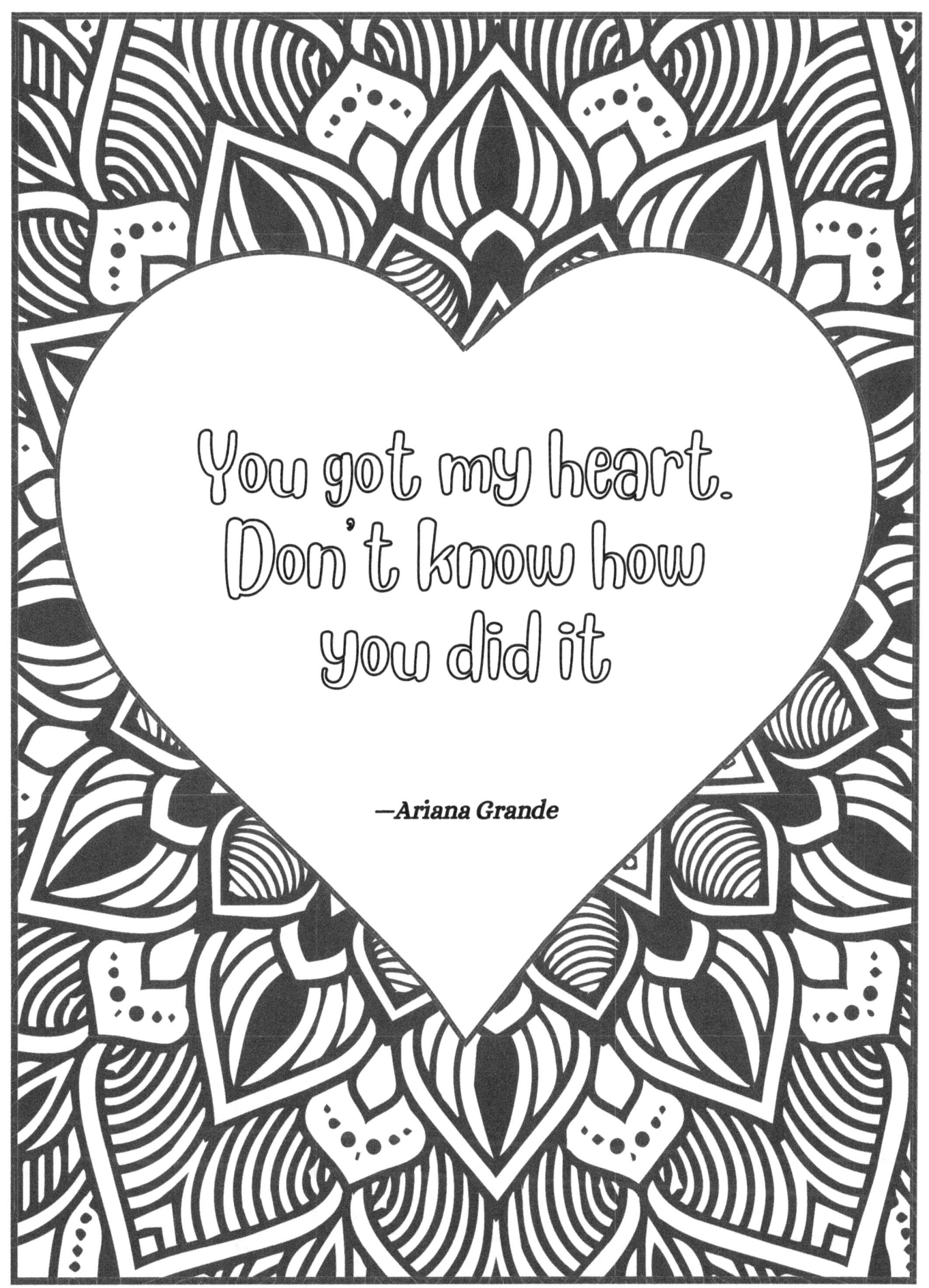

You got my heart. Don't know how you did it

—*Ariana Grande*

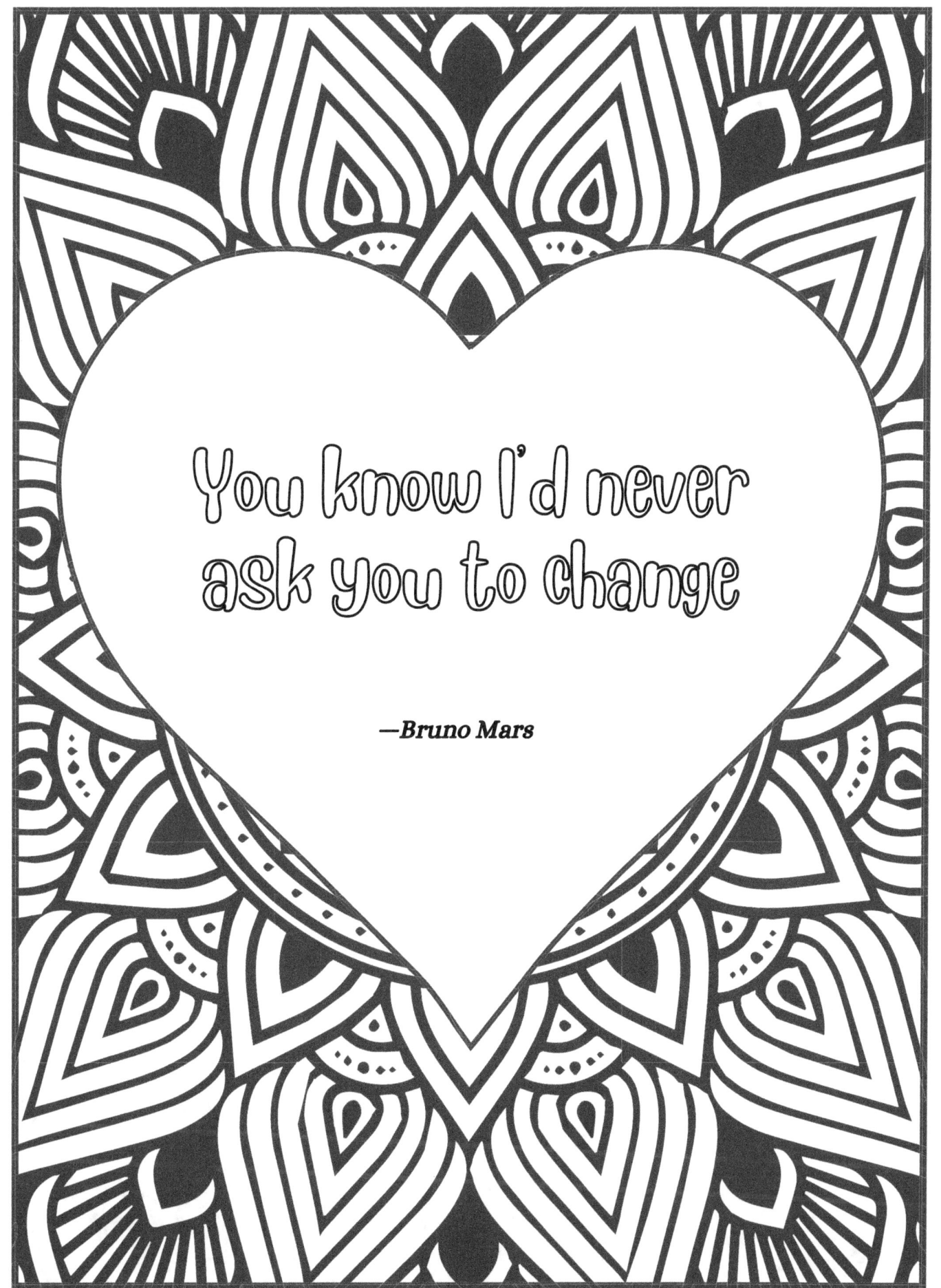

You know I'd never ask you to change

—*Bruno Mars*

You showed me a power that is strong enough to bring sun to the darkest days

—Harry Styles

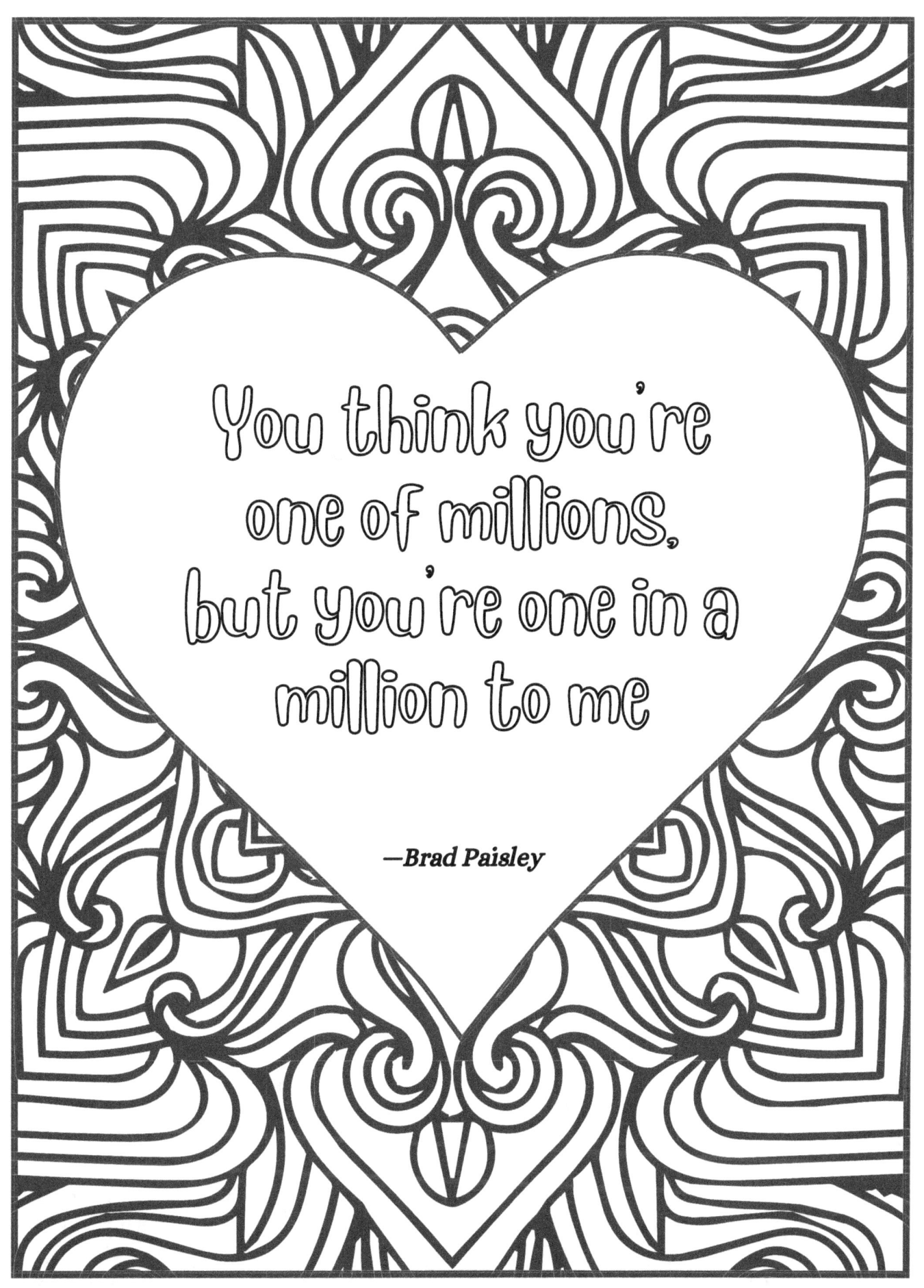

You're amazing. Just the way you are

—Bruno Mars

You've got the best of my love

—*The Emotions*

A Gift for You

Please join our mailing list to receive periodic updates and materials. You'll also be able to keep abreast of our future publications.

If you enjoy this book kindly check out Camptys Inspirations' range of coloring books, journals, activity books, and logs on Amazon and wherever you buy your books. Please remember to leave us a review.

As a thank you please scan the QR code to download a set of original inspirational posters that you can print, frame, and position in your favorite space.

http://eepurl.com/h8SU31

Other Books from the Author

REFLECTIONS
Inspirational Coloring Journal for Women

REFLECTIONS
Inspirational Coloring Journal for Teenage Boys

REFLECTIONS
Inspirational Coloring Journal for Men

REFLECTIONS
Inspirational Coloring Journal for Adults

A range of guided and gratitude journals

A range of Activity Books

A selection of Log Books

Inspirational Coloring Book for Teenage Girls

Inspirational Coloring Book for Teenage Boys

Inspirational Coloring Book for Women

Inspirational Coloring Book for Men

Inspirational Coloring Book for Adults

Inspirational Coloring Book for Boys 6-12

Inspirational Coloring Book for Girls 6-12

Coloring book for kids aged 4-8

Coloring book for kids aged 2-4

A Gift for You

Please join our mailing list to receive periodic updates and materials. You'll also be able to keep abreast of our future publications.

If you enjoy this book kindly check out Camptys Inspirations' range of coloring books, journals, activity books, and logs on Amazon and wherever you buy your books. Please remember to leave us a review.

As a thank you please scan the QR code to download a set of original inspirational posters that you can print, frame, and position in your favorite space.

http://eepurl.com/h8SU31

Other Books from the Author

REFLECTIONS
Inspirational Coloring Journal for Women

REFLECTIONS
Inspirational Coloring Journal for Teenage Boys

REFLECTIONS
Inspirational Coloring Journal for Men

REFLECTIONS
Inspirational Coloring Journal for Adults

A range of guided and gratitude journals

A range of Activity Books

A selection of Log Books

Inspirational Coloring Book for Teenage Girls

Inspirational Coloring Book for Teenage Boys

Inspirational Coloring Book for Women

Inspirational Coloring Book for Men

Inspirational Coloring Book for Adults

Inspirational Coloring Book for Boys 6-12

Inspirational Coloring Book for Girls 6-12

Coloring book for kids aged 4-8

Coloring book for kids aged 2-4